Also by Jimmy Carter

Christmas in Plains

An Hour Before Daylight

The Virtues of Aging

Sources of Strength: Meditations on Scripture for a Living Faith

Living Faith

The Little Baby Snoogle-Fleejer
(illustrated by Amy Carter)

Always a Reckoning, and Other Poems

Talking Peace: A Vision for the Next Generation

Turning Point: A Candidate, a State, and a Nation Come of Age

An Outdoor Journal: Adventures and Reflections

Everything to Gain: Making the Most of the Rest of Your Life
(with Rosalynn Carter)

The Blood of Abraham: Insights into the Middle East

Negotiation: The Alternative to Hostility

Keeping Faith: Memoirs of a President

A Government As Good As Its People

Why Not the Best?

THE
NOBEL
PEACE PRIZE
LECTURE

Delivered in Oslo on the 10th of December 2002

JIMMY CARTER

Simon & Schuster

NEW YORK LONDON TORONTO SYDNEY SINGAPORE

SIMON & SCHUSTER
Rockefeller Center
1230 Avenue of the Americas
New York, NY 10020

Nobel lecture and citation copyright © 2002
by Nobel Foundation, Stockholm
All other material copyright © 2002 The Carter Center
All rights reserved, including the right of reproduction
in whole or in part in any form.

SIMON & SCHUSTER and colophon are registered trademarks of
Simon & Schuster, Inc.

For information about special discounts for bulk purchases,
please contact Simon & Schuster Special Sales at
1-800-456-6798 or business@simonandschuster.com

Designed by C. Linda Dingler

Manufactured in the United States of America

10   9   8   7   6   5   4   3   2   1

Library of Congress Cataloging-in-Publication Data is available.

ISBN 0-7432-5068-0

To my colleagues
at The Carter Center

CONTENTS

CITATION

Following is the complete text of the Norwegian Nobel Committee's announcement of the 2002 Nobel Peace Prize as distributed by the committee:

The Norwegian Nobel Committee has decided to award the Nobel Peace Prize for 2002 to Jimmy Carter, for his decades of untiring effort to find peaceful solutions to international conflicts, to advance democracy and human rights, and to promote economic and social development.

During his presidency (1977–1981), Carter's mediation was a vital contribution to the Camp David Accords between Israel and Egypt, in itself a great enough achievement to qualify for the Nobel Peace Prize. At a time when the cold war between East and West was still predominant, he placed renewed emphasis on the place of human rights in international politics.

Through his Carter Center, which celebrates its 20th anniversary in 2002, Carter has since his presidency undertaken very extensive and persevering conflict resolution on several continents. He has shown outstanding commitment to human rights, and has served as an observer at countless elections all over the world. He has worked hard on many fronts to fight tropical diseases and to bring about growth and progress in developing countries. Carter has thus been active in several of the problem areas that have figured prominently in the over one hundred years of Peace Prize history.

In a situation currently marked by threats of the use of power, Carter has stood by the principles that conflicts must as far as possible be resolved through mediation and international co-operation based on international law, respect for human rights, and economic development.

Oslo, October 11, 2002

ACCEPTANCE STATEMENT

I am deeply grateful for this honor. I want to thank the Nobel Committee and the many people at The Carter Center who have worked side by side with me and my wife, Rosalynn, to promote peace, health, and human rights.

People everywhere share the same dream of a caring international community that prevents war and oppression. During the past two decades, as Rosalynn and I traveled around the world for the work of our Center, my concept of human rights has grown to include not only the right to live in peace, but also to adequate health care, shelter, food, and to economic opportunity.

I hope this award reflects a universal acceptance and even embrace of this broad-based concept of human rights.

This honor serves as an inspiration not only to us, but also to suffering people around the world, and I accept it on their behalf.

October 11, 2002

At his death on December 10, 1896, Alfred Bernhard Nobel, the Swedish scientist who invented dynamite, endowed a fund from which the income was to be awarded annually to several recipients who "conferred the greatest benefit on mankind."

At that time, Sweden and Norway were united, and Nobel decided to divide the responsibilities for awarding the prizes. Organizations in Sweden were to choose honorees in the fields of chemistry, physics, medicine, and literature, and a Norwegian committee would award the annual prize for peace. The first awards were made in 1901 on the anniversary of Nobel's death, and in 1968 another Swedish Nobel prize was added in the field of economics.

Except for nineteen years when no selections were made, the Nobel prizes for peace have been given in Norway to ninety individuals. In addition, a number of awards have gone to the International Committee of the Red Cross, agencies of the United Nations, and to other organizations.

It has become obvious that the Nobel prizes are awarded for two basic purposes: to recognize past accomplishments of the laureates and to inspire future progress for peace and human rights.

AUTHOR'S NOTE

I am deeply honored to receive the Nobel Prize for Peace. I first became aware of this award in 1952, when Albert Schweitzer was recognized for his dedicated work in a remote village in Africa. The award became dramatically important for all Americans when it was given in 1964 to Martin Luther King, Jr.

The first Nobel laureates whom I knew personally were Anwar Sadat and Menachem Begin, honored after we concluded a peace agreement at Camp David in 1978. I was very happy for my friends, who made courageous decisions leading to the signing of an Egyptian-Israeli peace treaty that has never been violated by either side.

In awarding me the prize this year, the Nobel committee mentioned my role in the Camp David

Accords, but the primary achievements for which it was given are those of The Carter Center during the past twenty years. The monetary prize will enhance the Center's work, now in sixty-five of the poorest and most needy countries on earth, where we continue to wage peace, fight disease, and build hope among our suffering neighbors around the world.

JIMMY CARTER

THE NOBEL PEACE PRIZE LECTURE

Your Majesties, Members of the Norwegian Nobel Committee, Excellencies, Ladies and Gentlemen:

It is with a deep sense of gratitude that I accept this prize. I am grateful to my wife, Rosalynn, to my colleagues at The Carter Center, and to many others who continue to seek an end to violence and suffering throughout the world. The scope and character of our Center's activities are perhaps unique, but in many other ways they are typical of the work being done by many hundreds of non-governmental organizations that strive for human rights and peace.

Most Nobel laureates have carried out our work in safety, but there are others who have acted with great personal courage. None has provided more vivid reminders of the dangers of peacemaking than two of my friends, Anwar Sadat and Yitzhak Rabin, who gave their lives for the cause of peace in the Middle East.

Like these two heroes, my first chosen career was in the military, as a submarine officer. My shipmates and I realized that we had to be ready to fight if combat was forced upon us, and we were prepared to give our lives to defend our nation and its principles. At the same time, we always prayed fervently that our readiness would ensure that there would be no war.

Later, as President and as Commander-in-Chief of our armed forces, I was one of those who bore the sobering responsibility of maintaining global stability during the height of the Cold War, as the world's two superpowers confronted each other. Both sides understood that an unresolved political altercation or a serious misjudgment could lead to a nuclear holocaust. In Washington and in

Moscow, we knew that we would have less than a half hour to respond after we learned that intercontinental missiles had been launched against us. There had to be a constant and delicate balancing of our great military strength with aggressive diplomacy, always seeking to build friendships with other nations, large and small, that shared a common cause.

In those days, the nuclear and conventional armaments of the United States and the Soviet Union were almost equal, but democracy ultimately prevailed because of commitments to freedom and human rights, not only by people in my country and those of our allies, but in the former Soviet empire as well. As President, I extended my public support and encouragement to Andrei Sakharov, who, although denied the right to attend the ceremony, was honored here for his personal commitments to these same ideals.

THE WORLD has changed greatly since I left the White House. Now there is only one superpower, with unprecedented military and economic strength. The coming budget for American armaments will be greater than those of the next fifteen nations combined, and there are troops from the United States in many countries throughout the world. Our gross national economy exceeds that of the three countries that follow us, and our nation's voice most often prevails as decisions are made concerning trade, humanitarian assistance, and the allocation of global wealth. This dominant status is unlikely to change in our lifetimes.

Great American power and responsibility are not unprecedented and have been used with restraint and great benefit in the past. We have not assumed that super strength guarantees super wisdom, and we have consistently reached out to the international community to ensure that our own power and influence are tempered by the best common judgment.

Within our country, ultimate decisions are made through democratic means, which tend to moderate radical or ill-advised proposals. Constrained and inspired by historic constitutional principles, our nation has endeavored for more than two hundred years to follow the now almost universal ideals of freedom, human rights, and justice for all.

Our President, Woodrow Wilson, was honored here for promoting the League of Nations, whose two basic concepts were profoundly important: "collective security" and "self-determination." Now they are embedded in international law. Violations of these premises during the last half-century have been tragic failures, as was vividly demonstrated when the Soviet Union attempted to conquer Afghanistan and when Iraq invaded Kuwait.

After the Second World War, American Secretary of State Cordell Hull received this prize for his role in founding the United Nations. His successor, General George C. Marshall, was recognized because of his efforts to help rebuild Europe, without excluding the vanquished nations of Italy and Germany. This was a historic example of respecting human rights at the international level.

Ladies and gentlemen:

Twelve years ago, President Mikhail Gorbachev received your recognition for his preeminent role in ending the Cold War that had lasted fifty years.

But instead of entering a millennium of peace, the world is now, in many ways, a more dangerous place. The greater ease of travel and communication has not been matched by equal understanding and mutual respect. There is a plethora of civil wars, unrestrained by rules of the Geneva Convention, within which an overwhelming portion of the casualties are unarmed civilians who have no ability to defend themselves. And recent appalling acts of terrorism have reminded us that no nations, even superpowers, are invulnerable.

It is clear that global challenges must be met with an emphasis on peace, in harmony with others, with strong alliances and international consensus. Imperfect as it may be, there is no doubt that this can best be done through the United Nations, which Ralph Bunche described here in this same forum as exhibiting a "fortunate flexibility"—not merely to preserve peace but also to make change, even radical change, without violence.

He went on to say: "To suggest that war can prevent war is a base play on words and a despicable form of warmongering. The objective of any who sincerely believe in peace clearly must be to exhaust every honorable recourse in the effort to save the peace. The world has had ample evidence that war begets only conditions that beget further war."

We must remember that today there are at least eight nuclear powers on earth, and three of them are threatening to their neighbors in areas of great international tension. For powerful countries to adopt a principle of preventive war may well set an example that can have catastrophic consequences.

IF WE ACCEPT the premise that the United Nations is the best avenue for the maintenance of peace, then the carefully considered decisions of the United Nations Security Council must be enforced. All too often, the alternative has proven to be uncontrollable violence and expanding spheres of hostility.

For more than half a century, following the founding of the State of Israel in 1948, the Middle East conflict has been a source of worldwide tension. At Camp David in 1978 and in Oslo in 1993, Israelis, Egyptians, and Palestinians have endorsed the only reasonable prescription for peace: United Nations Resolution 242. It condemns the acquisition of territory by force, calls for withdrawal of Israel from the occupied territories, and provides for Israelis to live securely and in harmony with their neighbors. There is no other mandate whose implementation could more profoundly improve international relationships.

Perhaps of more immediate concern is the necessity for Iraq to comply fully with the unanimous decision of the Security Council that it eliminate all weapons of mass destruction and permit unimpeded access by inspectors to confirm that this commitment has been honored. The world insists that this be done.

I THOUGHT often during my years in the White House of an admonition that we received in our small school in Plains, Georgia, from a beloved teacher, Miss Julia Coleman. She often said: "We must adjust to changing times and still hold to unchanging principles."

When I was a young boy, this same teacher also introduced me to Leo Tolstoy's novel *War and Peace*. She interpreted that powerful narrative as a reminder that the simple human attributes of goodness and truth can overcome great power. She also taught us that an individual is not swept along on a tide of inevitability but can influence even the greatest human events.

These premises have been proven by the lives of many heroes, some of whose names were little known outside their own regions until they became Nobel laureates: Albert John Lutuli, Norman Borlaug, Desmond Tutu, Elie Wiesel, Aung San Suu Kyi, Jody Williams, and even Albert Schweitzer and Mother Teresa. All of these and others have proven that even without government power—and often in opposition to it—individuals can enhance human rights and wage peace, actively and effectively.

The Nobel Prize also profoundly magnified the inspiring global influence of Martin Luther King, Jr., the greatest leader that my native state has ever produced. On a personal note, it is unlikely that my political career beyond Georgia would have been possible without the changes brought about by the civil rights movement in the American south and throughout our nation.

On the steps of our memorial to Abraham Lincoln, Dr. King said: "I have a dream that on the red hills of Georgia the sons of former slaves and the sons of former slave owners will be able to sit down together at a table of brotherhood."

The scourge of racism has not been vanquished, either in the red hills of our state or around the world. And yet we see ever more frequent manifestations of his dream of racial healing. In a symbolic but very genuine way, at least involving two Georgians, it is coming true in Oslo today.

I AM NOT here as a public official, but as a citizen of a troubled world who finds hope in a growing consensus that the generally accepted goals of society are peace, freedom, human rights, environmental quality, the alleviation of suffering, and the rule of law.

During the past decades, the international community, usually under the auspices of the United Nations, has struggled to negotiate global standards that can help us achieve these essential goals. They include: the abolition of land mines and chemical weapons; an end to the testing, proliferation, and further deployment of nuclear warheads; constraints on global warming; prohibition of the death penalty, at least for children; and an international criminal court to deter and to punish war crimes and genocide. Those agreements already adopted must be fully implemented, and others should be pursued aggressively.

We must also strive to correct the injustice of economic sanctions that seek to penalize abusive leaders but all too often inflict punishment on those who are already suffering from the abuse.

THE UNCHANGING principles of life predate modern times. I worship Jesus Christ, whom we

Christians consider to be the Prince of Peace. As a Jew, he taught us to cross religious boundaries, in service and in love. He repeatedly reached out and embraced Roman conquerors, other Gentiles, and even the more despised Samaritans.

Despite theological differences, all great religions share common commitments that define our ideal secular relationships. I am convinced that Christians, Muslims, Buddhists, Hindus, Jews, and others can embrace each other in a common effort to alleviate human suffering and to espouse peace.

But the present era is a challenging and disturbing time for those whose lives are shaped by religious faith based on kindness toward each other. We have been reminded that cruel and inhuman acts can be derived from distorted theological beliefs, as suicide bombers take the lives of innocent human beings, draped falsely in the cloak of God's will. With horrible brutality, neighbors have massacred neighbors in Europe, Asia, and Africa.

In order for us human beings to commit ourselves personally to the inhumanity of war, we find it necessary first to dehumanize our opponents, which is in itself a violation of the beliefs of all religions. Once we characterize our adversaries as beyond the scope of God's mercy and grace, their lives lose all value. We deny personal responsibility when we plant land mines and, days or years later, a stranger to us—often a child—is crippled or killed. From a great distance, we launch bombs or missiles with almost total impunity and never want to know the number or identity of the victims.

At the beginning of this new millennium I was asked to discuss, here in Oslo, the greatest challenge that the world faces. Among all the possible choices, I decided that the most serious and universal problem is the growing chasm between the richest and poorest people on earth. Citizens of the ten wealthiest countries are now seventy-five times richer than those who live in the ten poorest ones, and the separation is increasing every year, not only between nations but also within them. The results of this disparity are root causes of most of the world's unresolved problems, including starvation, illiteracy, environmental degradation, violent conflict, and unnecessary illnesses that range from Guinea worm to HIV/AIDS.

Most work of The Carter Center is in remote villages in the poorest nations of Africa, and there I have witnessed the capacity of destitute people to persevere under heartbreaking conditions. I have come to admire their judgment and wisdom, their courage and faith, and their awesome accomplishments when given a chance to use their innate abilities.

But tragically, in the industrialized world there is a terrible absence of understanding or concern about those who are enduring lives of despair and hopelessness. We have not yet made the commitment to share with others an appreciable part of our excessive wealth. This is a potentially rewarding burden that we should all be willing to assume.

Ladies and gentlemen:

War may sometimes be a necessary evil. But no matter how necessary, it is always an evil, never a good. We will not learn how to live together in peace by killing each other's children.

The bond of our common humanity is stronger than the divisiveness of our fears and prejudices. God gives us the capacity for choice. We can choose to alleviate suffering. We can choose to work together for peace. We can make these changes—and we must.

Thank you.

Oslo, December 10, 2002